A FAMILY RESTAURANT IS NO PLACE FOR CHILDREN

The Wit and Wisdom of an Uncommon Mom

as complied by Steve Liddick

A FAMILY RESTAURANT IS NO PLACE FOR CHILDREN

The Wit and Wisdom of an Uncommon Mom

as complied by Steve Liddick

TOP CAT PUBLICATIONS

A FAMILY RESTAURANT IS NO PLACE FOR CHILDREN:
THE WIT AND WISDOM OF AN UNCOMMON MOM

Printed in the United States of America for Worldwide Distribution
ISBN# 978-0-9991575-7-2

Dedicated to the memory of Ruth E. Liddick
(Mom)

A FAMILY RESTAURANT
IS NO PLACE FOR CHILDREN:
THE WIT AND WISDOM OF AN UNCOMMON MOM

as compiled by Steve Liddick

There is the mistaken notion that all wisdom is already out there, written and spoken by famous people long ago, as though everyday folks never came up with anything worth remembering—and certainly not lately.

Well, here's a news item for you. As you will see, my mother said some pretty wise stuff in her time. "Out of the mouths of babes," as they say. Mom was one babe who spun her philosophy at home where it would do some good. While all those dead guys were out there, carving their words into granite, Mom was aiming her wisdom at her kids and her friends.

Maybe they ran out of granite or something because you don't see a lot of that anymore.

Today you will find a lot of worthwhile philosophy on office cubicle walls, bumper stickers, T-shirts, emails, photocopies circulated around the office, Internet social media sites, and coffee table books. Lots more than there ever were on all the public buildings and cave walls put together. I have to say, though, that most office photocopies that are funny are usually too dirty to send to your mother. But, if you want to know the truth, my Mom would probably have laughed her butt off at those. In fact, she came up with some pretty hot stuff of her own over the years.

Mom's wisdom leaned more toward observations of others as examples of what her kids should—or should not—do and be. Bits of insight that serve me best in my own life are those I learned at my mother's knee—the original knee, not the one the surgeons replaced it with in 1993.

Considering the energy level of her rowdy offspring, Mom's methods of child rearing might more accurately be described as "crowd control." Still, all three of us have managed to be duly employed, have not become—nor do we hang out with—felons, politicians, or other unsavory characters. We are kind to animals, read a book a week, look both ways before crossing the street, chew one-hundred times before swallowing, never sit in a draft, always wear a sweater when we go out so we don't catch our death of cold, never eat anything sold by a street vendor because it could kill you, always wear clean underwear in case—God forbid—we should get into an accident, and, like good scouts, we are cheerful, thrifty, brave, clean and reverent.

Well, maybe not 'reverent', when you consider our role model.

Mom suffered no fools, gladly or otherwise; sacred cows slaughtered while you wait. She didn't mellow much over the years with regard to the suffering of fools. And all the way into her final years she was still the same imaginative, fiercely loyal, honest, kind, fun-loving, card-playing, spunky old broad I had always known. She was the yardstick by which I will always measure everyone else.

I remember one particular incident on a visit to Florida. My plane arrived at Tampa International Airport early in the morning. It was that time of the day when most people, myself included, had a fur coat on their tongues and could barely eat or drink anything without gagging. Mom was in her car, waiting for me outside the terminal. I tossed my luggage in the trunk and slid into the passenger seat. Between us was a beverage cooler.

"You want a beer?" she said.

"Mom!" I said. "It's only 7:30 in the morning!"

"I didn't ask you what time it was," she said with a snort. "I asked you if you wanted a beer."

While that occasion may not qualify as wisdom—exactly—I think it demonstrates very nicely the thinking processes of this person who has affected my life so dramatically.

Mom's wisdom usually came with a dash of humor; just enough to get the message across without losing the serious intent. I once offered to buy her a welcome mat with a smiling cartoon figure on it. She declined, saying "I put that outside my door, salesmen might think I meant *them*."

Humor coupled with wisdom may have some drawbacks.

"If you say something wise, people think you're smart," Mom said. "If you say something wise and funny, people think you're a smart ass." See? The woman's wisdom just keeps on coming.

If you want to be a pilot you have to undergo a rigorous training period. It takes a lot of sweat, skill and expense to learn to fly an airplane. It's pretty much the same for every discipline that imposes great responsibility: the practice of medicine, becoming a police officer, teaching school, etc. On the other hand, any pair of hormone-fueled adolescents can produce a child without a lick of training. I suppose when Mom started out she probably didn't know any more than most people about raising children. But some mothers are naturals. If there was an NBA of parents, Mom would have been on the All-Star team.

Mothers are *expected* to be wise. I happen to be one of the lucky ones whose mother actually *was*.

With everything that life had slammed up against her, neither Mom's wit nor wisdom suffered. It must have done us kids some good because, as Adolf Hitler was often heard to say, "Look at me, I turned out okay, didn't I?"

By the time Mom was a teenager, the Great Depression had ripped through the nation, her hometown, her neighborhood, and her family.

Mom was one of five children. My grandfather was fortunate to have a job through those terrible economic times. Before he became a railroad engineer, he started as a fireman on the old Pennsylvania Railroad, shoveling coal into steam locomotive fireboxes for $11 a week at a time when other heads of families were selling apples on the street for nickels and worrying themselves into early graves. Still, Grandma clothed and fed her kids and made meals out of not much of anything.

Troubling times inspire more greatness than prosperous times. If Michelangelo'd had a smooth childhood, there would probably be no Pieta. The Sistine Chapel ceiling would very likely be painted with Sherwin-

Williams off-white and the Vatican's hallways would probably be lined with pictures of Popes on velvet. The period we call "The Renaissance" might simply be referred to as "way back when."

Mom's family's difficulties and their skill at overcoming them created some of the best people I've ever known.

Her early education in hard times prepared her not only for making the best of what she had, but for the tough job of raising three spirited children (read that: "terrorists") of her own. Even when she had to deprive herself, Diane, Paul and I came first. Of course, we didn't know that at the time. We didn't know how hard it was to keep things together because Mom kept it to herself and let us concentrate on being kids.

Ruth E. Liddick was born on January 17th, 1916. She left us on October 9th, 2008, just 100 days short of her 93rd birthday. But she left behind some great memories and a roadmap to the future.

We knew that she was a really smart, funny, irreverent lady who kept us laughing and made us think. We find we are still capable of that today.

Mom was only 22-years older than I. In a way, we kind of grew up together. Then we grew old together.

It was a wonderful trip.

Following are some of the things we carry around in our heads and hearts.

And it's all her fault.

Steve Liddick, eldest son of Ruth Erma (Kiner) Liddick (1916 –2008)

MOM'S
WIT
AND
WISDOM

MOM'S WIT AND WISDOM

Anyone who doesn't believe in zombies has
never noticed the other shoppers at Walmart.

Formal dining is any restaurant
where the waitresses are not on roller skates.

I'll overlook your flaws
if you'll forgive my perfection.

Grinning and bearing it takes
a lot out of a person.

If Abraham Lincoln had not been assassinated in 1865, he'd probably be dead now anyway.

When I become Queen, everything will be different.

For getting your own way, nothing is quite as effective as a bad reputation.

When push comes to shove, shove usually wins.

Dear Lord, we pray that you protect us from experts.

Sometimes a bad example is the best example.

If the meek inherit the earth,
they aren't likely to stay meek.

Self-confidence often results from a lack of experience.
Maybe that explains teenagers.

Another day, another dither.

The only thing I'm sure of is that
there's not much you can be sure of.

If I don't get my way pretty soon
there's going to be a revolution.

True joy is discovering there is
a full page of comics I haven't read yet.

You can't have everything. Why is that?

If the shoe fits, wear it
and stop bellyaching.

If you have to have a stroke,
a stroke of genius is the best kind.

You can be supremely confident
by always assuming the other person is wrong.

The future starts right now.
What are you waiting for?

Never tell your enemies
what they're doing wrong.

Fishing is the art of doing *nothing*
while seeming to be doing *something*.

Staying angry is hard work.

Every time I figure out an answer to one of life's important questions, I come up with ten more questions.

Good times build strong economies.
Hard times build strong character.

Anyone can be a friend when it doesn't cost them anything.

You can tell a lot about a person's character by whether they return the jar you gave them homemade jelly in.

Everyone is irritating sometimes.

People will always disappoint you until
you accept that humans are human.

Set high standards for yourself,
and don't let anyone talk you out of them.

You can't start improving yourself
any sooner than right now.

If they can put a man on the moon, why can't they keep my favorite comic strip off the fold of the newspaper?

There is a lot to be said for a dull life.

Get right to it; keep right at it.

Don't confuse *Dreams* with *Plans*.

The most dangerous animal in the world
is a person with nothing to lose.

Humor is often anger turned constructive.

We laugh at jokes, but someone
always gets hurt.

Humor is nothing to be taken lightly.

Any fool can tell you
how an idea will *NOT* work.

I don't know why they call it "common" sense.
Good sense isn't all that common.

I can do a lot with very little
but I can't do everything with nothing.

Patience is not an emotion, it is a procedure.

Power is not *given*, it is *taken*.

After all is said and done, much has been said
and little has been done.

Be careful who you treat like a nobody.
They may turn out to be somebody.

Having an incorrect crossword
puzzle answer is bad enough.
Being wrong in *INK* is a tragedy.

Beware of unsolicited favors. The giver may want them repaid in inconvenient installments.

Worse than hating your job
is not having one.

Never miss an opportunity
to keep your mouth shut.

Sooner or later every fool is found out.

Prosperity comes to those
who overcome their fear of success.

Dreading an unpleasant chore usually
takes more energy than the chore, itself.

Do the least pleasant job on your list first.

Most people are good.
Mostly due to lack of opportunity.

Emotional wounds can't be healed with logic.

Some of the most intelligent people I know
aren't very smart sometimes.

You can make something
out of nothing if you have all the stuff.

If we had any bacon I'd fix bacon and eggs
if we had any eggs.

Being curious is no excuse to embarrass.

It's kinder to ignore some faults.

If you take up a musical instrument,
be sure it's one you put in your mouth
so you won't be tempted to sing.

All you can do is all you can do.

Those who can't achieve fame
often settle for notoriety.

Dreams are the mind's way
of working things out.

Hating someone is harder
than trying to figure them out.

People are more alike
than they are different from each other.

Even if you love your job
it's okay to still be glad for Fridays.

Sometimes the simplest way is the best way.

Never slam a door in a house full of cats.

Never miss a chance to make someone happy.
Even if you have to leave town to do it.

Workaholics aren't working. They're playing.

There's nothing like a change of perspective
to ruin the old one you've learned to live with.

Repayment for a good deed received,
is a lifetime of good deeds given.

Don't complain about an offense someone has committed that you
have also committed—if only once. This may be their "once".

At times we are all guilty
of what we dislike in others.

Being an American is my reward
for being good in a previous life.

A blind man knows true beauty when he hears it.

Justice often comes to those who can't afford it.

It doesn't take all kinds to make a world.
Just the same, we *have* all kinds.

Misery may love company, but it won't have mine.

Comfortable people are the least reliable of all.

Don't be afraid of what evil people
are *capable* of doing. Be afraid
of what they are *willing* to do.

Every day gets better if we work at it.

Never say anything behind someone's
back you wouldn't say to their face.

Sometimes "control freaks" are simply
people who are afraid of surprises.

Anything that might be important later
has to be treated as important *now*.

It's the little successes that keep us going.

There are things I'll do for nothing
that I wouldn't do for anyone
for any amount of money.

If learning to read is the foundation of education,
learning logic and ethics is the foundation for life.

You can't get ahead by
staying in the slow lane.

Give most people an easier
choice and they'll take it.

When cars get 200 miles to a gallon of gas,
a gallon of gas will cost 200-dollars.

Anyone who will lie to you
will also steal from you.

You can't fail if you don't try.
You also can't succeed.

I never respond to questions asked by people
who aren't entitled to an answer.

Yell at the guy you're mad at,
not the guy closest to you.

Don't spoil your weekend because
you're dreading Monday.

People often judge you by what you think of yourself.

If you're good at one thing,
people tend to believe
you're good at everything.

You can't change some things that have
happened. All you can do is go from here.

It's never too late to have a nice day.

Human nature is a wonderful—and terrible—thing.

When the boss stops caring about the employees,
the employees stop caring about the job.

Things don't work out. You have to work things out.

Sometimes the light at the end of the
tunnel is an oncoming freight train.

Everywhere you go you take yourself with you.

I spend half the time fretting about the past
and half the time worrying about the future.
I let the other half take care of itself.

Anyone can like someone everyone likes.
The challenge is to find the good
in those hardly anyone likes.

Silence is often an opinion.

Why is a *woman* who cooks called a "cook" and
a *man* who cooks is called a "gourmet chef?"

A cook is someone who prepares food.
A *chef* is someone who prepares food
and places a sprig of rosemary on top.

Perfection is an impossible goal,
so let's just try to do the best we can.

No matter where you live,
there is some kind of natural disaster
to make life difficult.

Everyone is a genius at something.

If we couldn't laugh at life,
we'd probably sit right down and cry.

The really important lessons in life
are usually learned the hard way.

Even people who prefer being
alone sometimes get lonely.

The best gift you can give a person
is to help them to succeed.

It's a short distance between
confidence and arrogance.

An occasional challenge to our comfort
is a good lesson in perspective.

People don't value something
that doesn't cost them anything.

To be trusted is an honor.

No matter what you do in life, there's
always someone who will tell you
how you should have done it.

If everything we ate came in a pill,
no one would be overweight.

If you have succeeded, it may be because
you didn't know it couldn't be done.

Everyone needs an occasional
humbling experience.

What means nothing to you may
mean everything to someone else.

Pretension: It's absolutely everywhere, dahling!

If the week seems longer than the
weekend, that's because it is.

It takes effort to be a good friend.

Those who try to get all of it
often end up with none of it.

TV news and the Internet are replacing
newspapers. I fear for the Republic.

Golf is another form of insanity.

Substitute absence for patience.
Walk away and come back later.

There's always a tomorrow
to put things off until.

If we think a flea is small,
what must a flea think is small?

If you don't stay alert,
life can really bite you in the ass.

I have found that self pity is entirely portable.
I can take it with me wherever I go.

If you call and somebody other than me answers
the phone, tell them to get the hell out of my house.

I have some home exercise equipment
and I think I know where it is.

I don't hate exercising. I'd even be willing
to pay someone to do it for me.

We often use humor like radar,
sending out signals to see what bounces back.

I get nervous when my enemies agree with me.

Some occupations are too important to hire
a person just because they want the job.

A clever idea is not always a good idea.

Everyone is at least a little crazy. It's what
we do with our craziness that counts.

If we weren't a little crazy we'd probably go nuts.

One-percent of the people
cause 99-percent of the trouble.

Logic may recognize boundaries,
but emotion is the wide open spaces.

Don't treat everyone like the worst one.

A banana is room-temperature ice cream.

More games are lost because of the loser's
mistakes than the winner's skill.

Nothing is more damaging than having
too many people approve of you.

Comfort is the enemy of thought.

If you always wait until tomorrow
to do the important things, you probably
won't do them tomorrow either.

Today is yesterday's *tomorrow*.
What have you done toward *today's* tomorrow?

Mark Twain used the same words we all do,
but look what he did with them.

I considered learning Latin,
but who would I talk to?

Nobody is allowed to yell at
you on your birthday.

Paranoia has saved more lives than the American Red Cross.

I've done just about everything. Anything
I do now will just be repeating myself.

Things are so slow around here, even the
motion detector isn't picking up anything.

Less is more sometimes. Except
if we're talking about ice cream.

The things we get for free
can sometimes end up being very expensive.

When it comes to reaching your goals,
persistence is often better than intelligence.

It is a brave person who challenges a friend,
and a brave friend who appreciates the challenge.

Democracy is at the awkward age.
And always will be.

There's no such thing as an ugly dog.

No more coffee for me
or I won't be able to sleep all day.

In Congress, compromise means "do it my way."

Education is a cumulative process.
Miss a day of school and you
have missed a link in the chain.

When the going gets tough, the tough bake cookies.

Most of what I know I learned by accident.

Luck is actually hard work in disguise.

I wake up at 5 a.m., but my brain doesn't wake up until 11.

People who don't really want a job
are experts at not getting one.

If you wait around to see what happens,
things are more likely to happen *to* you
than *for* you.

Be patient. You haven't made
all of your mistakes yet.

Life's lasting lessons are not learned
at our mother's knee, but *over* her knee.

Sometimes you have to stand way back
to get a closer look at your life.

Do everything the best you can
and the rest of your life will take care of itself.

Today is better than yesterday was,
but not as good as tomorrow will be.

SOME PEOPLE

SOME PEOPLE

For some people, the heaviest load
they bear is to hold their tongue.

Some people mistake *Style* for *Class*.

Some people who rock the boat
should spend more time rowing it.

Some people let their brains go to their head.

I have very little patience with people
who have very little patience.

People who say "to be perfectly
honest with you" seldom are.

People who steal ideas rarely have any of their own.

Some people don't know they don't know everything
so they assume that everything they do know
is everything.

Some people work harder at getting out of work than most people work at *working*.

Some people who think they are truffles are actually toadstools.

Some people mistake being "appointed" for being "anointed".

What some people call "frankness" in themselves, they call "meanness" in others.

If not for a sense of humor,
some people wouldn't have any sense at all.

It takes some people a half hour
to get ready for a ten minute work break.

Some people should never
be given any authority.

Some people would lie even if the truth
would get them out of quicksand.

Some people will think you're a genius
and some will think you're a fool.
Don't take either too seriously.

If not for exercises in futility, some people
would never get any exercise at all.

Why do some people take pride in their bad temper?

Some people find faults in others
to distract from their own.

Some people tell their pets they love them more often than they say it to their spouse and kids.

When some people ask for advice, what they really want is approval for what they already plan to do.

Some people have to die to go to Hell. Others find it at a job they hate.

Some people spend more time looking
for those who agree with them than
they spend looking for the facts.

Some people believe if you don't know
the same things they know, you must be stupid.

Why do some people's confidence
outrun their competence?

For some people, their most terrifying
moment is a lull in the conversation.

FRIENDSHIP, LOVE AND SEX

FRIENDSHIP, LOVE, AND SEX

It's been so long since I've sinned,
the statute of limitations has run out.

A libido is a terrible thing to waste.

Just because you get old doesn't mean it goes away.

If she's a nice girl she won't care
what kind of car you drive.

Everyone needs someone
to worry about them.

Good friends are too precious
to handle carelessly.

Relying heavily on someone can often
be mistaken for being taken for granted.

There's a lot more to homosexuals than sex.

Everybody needs somebody
to believe they are Number One.

Ugly ducklings make the best swans.

It's not reasonable to assume
that you are your best friend's best friend.

To most women, sex is a commitment.
To most men, sex is a sport.

MONEY

MONEY

If you think Halloween is scary,
try living on Social Security.

Working for a living sure
takes up a lot of your day.

Everybody's got to make a living.
Even the fly that lands on your pie.

Never say "only" when you're
talking about money.

Little amounts add up to big amounts
if there are enough little amounts.

Money can't buy happiness, but it
can provide a better kind of misery.

Saving your money today gives you a wonderful
opportunity to waste it tomorrow.

Don't get so busy trying to make a killing
that you forget to make a living.

Whoever said "money can't buy happiness"
ought to try being poor sometime.

Live cheap, die rich.

Having a lot of money does not
necessarily mean you are rich.

The money you make on top of the money you make
is where you make your money.

Here I am, living in
the lap of poverty.

People with money do not always have class,
and people with all the class in the world can be dead broke

Why is government money that comes
to *our* congressional district is called "federal funding,"
while money that goes to other districts is called "pork?"

RETIREMENT,

OLD AGE, . . .

AND BEYOND

RETIREMENT, OLD AGE . . . AND BEYOND

God made weekends to let people
practice for retirement.

My mirror is a dirty, rotten liar.

I'm so old that all my dreams
are in black and white.

I no longer judge age by the number of years behind me,
but by the denomination of money I would
no longer stoop down to pick up.

People will have to love me for my mind
because my body is shot to hell.

It's a good thing to marry young.
Who would want someone who looks like this?

I remember the 1940s very well.
It's *yesterday* I have trouble with.

My thumbs don't twiddle as good as they used to.
But then, neither does anything else.

The good thing about being
young is that you get over it.
That's also the bad thing.

It's getting so when I change my mind
I forget what I changed it from.

Anything I eat now that will kill me in 30 years
is wasting its time.

The only antique around my house is me.
Everything else is just old.

Has anybody seen my youth?
It was around here a minute ago.

If I had more energy I'd go take a nap.

If you're only as old as you feel,
I must be chasing Methuselah's record.

Those who say age is just a number
usually have a low number.

When I was young they said I was "talented."
When I was middle aged they said I was "experienced."
Now that I'm old they say
I don't know that the hell I'm talking about.

If you want to know what it's like to be invisible,
just grow old—or ride a motorcycle.

I'm not afraid of the dead,
but some of the living
scare the hell out of me.

If I knew then what I know now,
then might not have been so bad.

Why is it I can't remember the things I need to know, but
I clearly recall every stupid thing I've ever said and done?

Being older gives you a bigger pile of things
you can kick yourself about.

Time plays some pretty mean tricks on you.

Vanity is the last thing to go.

Learning from our experiences is a good way
to avoid future problems, but learning from *other*
people's experiences saves a lot of time.

Life is a series of lessons.
If you're not a fast learner,
LOOK OUT!

The older I get, the younger 80-years-old seems.

The older I get, the less I know for sure.

The past has passed.
That's why they call it that.

Life is a work in progress.

If anyone ever offers you an unsolicited
senior citizen discount, just smack him.
Then take it.

I don't hurry as fast as I used to.

Retirement is a state of self-unemployment.

Learn from the past; Enjoy the present;
Plan for the future.

Time really flies when you're old.

The older I get, the more people
I tell to go to hell.

Life is a test. How do you think
you'll do on the final exam?

Gravity wins in the end.

Dying is like sleeping,
except you don't have to get up
in the middle of the night to go to the bathroom.

Promise me you won't let them
play bagpipes at my funeral.

Thanks, Mom

48796451R10056